P9-DHZ-905

BRAZIL
the people

Malika Hollander

A Bobbie Kalman Book

The Lands, Peoples, and Cultures Series

 Crabtree Publishing Company

www.crabtreebooks.com

LIBRARY
FRANKLIN PIERCE COLLEGE
RINDGE, NH 03461

The Lands, Peoples, and Cultures Series

Created by Bobbie Kalman

Coordinating editor
Ellen Rodger

Production coordinator
Rosie Gowsell

Project development, photo research, design, and editing
First Folio Resource Group, Inc.
  Erinn Banting
  Tom Dart
  Claire Milne
  Jaimie Nathan
  Debbie Smith

Prepress and printing
Worzalla Publishing Company

Consultants
Lêda Leitão Martins, Cornell University; John M. Norvell,
Cornell University

Photographs
AFP/Corbis/Magma: p. 24 (right); Mary Altier: p. 15 (bottom);
Archivo Iconografico, S.A./Corbis/Magma: p. 21;
Nair Benedicto, D. Donne Bryant Stock: p. 5 (bottom), p. 11
(left); Bettman/Corbis/Magma: p. 8 (right), page 9 (top and
bottom left); Cynthia Brito, D. Donne Bryant Stock: p. 18 (left);
Pierre Colombel/Corbis/Magma: p. 6; Marc Crabtree: cover,
title page, p. 4 (both), p. 5 (top), p. 14 (left), p. 15 (top), p. 16
(both), p. 17 (bottom), p. 18 (right), p. 22 (left), p. 23 (bottom),
p. 24 (left), p. 25, p. 26 (right), p. 27 (left), p. 28 (both), p. 29,
p. 30, p. 31 (left); Salomon Cytrynowicz, D. Donne Bryant
Stock: p. 20 (right); Monica Dalmasso/ImageState: p. 12;
Mark Downey/Lucid Images: p. 13 (bottom); Victor
Engelbert/Photo Researchers: p. 26 (left); Laurence
Fordyce/Corbis/Magma: p. 27 (right); Lois Ellen
Frank/Corbis/Magma: p. 3; Robert Fried: p. 20 (left);
Historical Picture Archive/Corbis/Magma: p. 8 (left); Hulton
Archive/Getty Images: p. 7 (bottom); Randall Hyman: p. 22
(right), p. 23 (top); Wolfgang Kaehler/Corbis/Magma: p. 10
(right), p. 19; Larry Luxner: p. 9 (right); Michael Moody, D.
Donne Bryant Stock: p. 14 (right), p. 31 (right); Michael
Nichols/ImageState: p. 13 (top); Saulo Petean, D. Donne
Bryant Stock: p. 10 (left); The Pierpont Morgan Library/Art
Resource, NY: p. 7 (top); Reuters NewMedia
Inc./Corbis/Magma: p. 11 (right)

Illustrations
Dianne Eastman: icon
David Wysotski, Allure Illustrations: back cover

Cover: A member of the Kayapó tribe, an indigenous group
from the Amazon rainforest.

Title page: A man from Rio de Janeiro does flips on the beach
as he enjoys Brazil's sunny weather.

Icon: Large ferryboats, called *gaiolas*, which appear at the
head of each section, carry passengers up and down the
Amazon River.

Back cover: The toco toucan lives in Brazil's rainforests. It uses
its large bill to snap up fruit on branches that are hard to reach.

All ready to go! Photographer Marc Crabtree spent several
weeks photographing Brazil for this book.

Published by
Crabtree Publishing Company

PMB 16A,   612 Welland Avenue   73 Lime Walk
350 Fifth Avenue   St. Catharines   Headington
Suite 3308   Ontario, Canada   Oxford OX3 7AD
New York   L2M 5V6   United Kingdom
N.Y. 10118

Copyright © **2003 CRABTREE PUBLISHING COMPANY**.
All rights reserved. No part of this publication may be
reproduced, stored in a retrieval system or transmitted in any
form or by any means, electronic, mechanical, photocopying,
recording, or otherwise, without the prior written permission
of Crabtree Publishing Company.

Cataloging-in-Publication Data
Hollander, Malika.
    Brazil. The people / Malika Hollander.
      p. cm. -- (Lands, peoples, and cultures)
    Includes index.
    Summary: Explores how the history, climate, geography, and
religion of Brazil have shaped the customs and practices of
modern daily life for some of the poorest and some of the
wealthiest people in South America.
    ISBN 0-7787-9339-7 (RLB) -- ISBN 0-7787-9707-4 (PB)
    1. Brazil--Social life and customs--Juvenile literature. 2.
Ethnicity--Brazil--Juvenile literature. [1. Brazil--Social life and
customs. 2. Ethnology--Brazil.] I. Title: People. II. Title. III.
Series: Lands, peoples, and cultures.
    F2510.H66 2003
    981--dc21
                                            2003001267
                                            LC

Contents

More than 80 percent of the people living in the northeastern city of Salvador have ancestors from Africa. The city's music, dance, and food reflect the people's African heritage.

Brazilians come from many backgrounds and practice a wide variety of customs. In Salvador, a city in the northeast, women who follow the African-Brazilian religion of Candomblé place candles on rafts and send them out to sea as offerings to the goddess Iemanjá. Deep in the Amazon rainforest, **indigenous** boys hunt lizards with bows and arrows. In the far south, Brazilian cowboys, called *gaúchos*, round up cattle on large ranches. In the southeastern city of Rio de Janeiro, soccer fans cheer on their favorite team in the world's largest soccer stadium, Maracanã. Together, these people make Brazil a lively, fascinating place.

Friends meet for a volleyball match on Flamengo Beach, in the southeastern city of Rio de Janeiro.

A shared language and religion

About 170 million people live in Brazil. This is almost half the population of South America. The Portuguese **colonized** Brazil for almost 300 years, bringing their language and religion with them. Today, Portuguese is Brazil's official language, but the version of Portuguese spoken in Brazil includes thousands of words from indigenous and African languages. Almost 90 percent of Brazilians are Roman Catholic, the main religion of Portugal. Many of these people combine Catholicism with other beliefs.

Endless riches

Brazil is a land of great beauty, with long coasts, jagged mountains, and wetlands and rainforests with wildlife found nowhere else in the world. The country's **fertile** soil and buried **natural resources** bring it great wealth, but Brazil has serious **economic** problems. The government has borrowed enormous sums of money from foreign banks to develop its industries, and has been unable to pay it back. As well, while a small number of Brazilians are very wealthy, many more live in great poverty. Bringing a good standard of living, including decent health care, education, and housing, to all Brazilians is one of the country's greatest challenges.

Soccer fans carrying Brazilian flags celebrate Brazil's World Cup soccer victory in 2002.

The Kayapó, who live in the Amazon rainforest, work hard to protect their land and customs. They earn a living without harming the environment, by gathering Brazil nuts, which are eaten or used to make soap, and by selling traditional crafts.

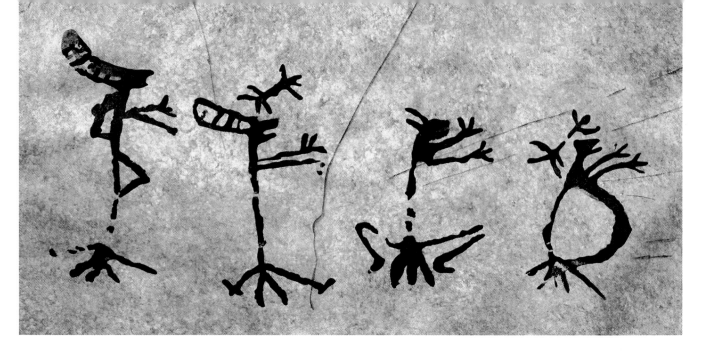

 # From colony to country

In 1988, a Brazilian teacher led an American **archaeologist** to see paintings of people and animals, red and yellow handprints, and geometric shapes on the walls of Caverna da Pedra Pintada, or Cave of the Painted Rocks, in the northern Amazon. Buried in the cave were spear points, knives made of stone, and the remains of fish, birds, turtles, fruit, and seeds. Brazilians had known that there were ancient spear points and other tools in the area, but they did not realize, as the archaeologist did, that they dated back 11,000 years, to the time of the first Brazilians.

The first Brazilians

The first Brazilians, the ancestors of today's indigenous people, crossed a land bridge from Asia to North America, then moved south to Brazil. Some settled in the Amazon and Atlantic rainforests, where they fished and farmed small plots of land. Others settled in the **plains** and **plateaus** of central and southern Brazil. There, they hunted, fished, and gathered food. When the Portuguese arrived in 1500, there were between two million and four million indigenous people.

Dividing the new world

In the late 1400s, explorers from Portugal and Spain were traveling the world, looking for goods to trade and land to claim as their own. In 1494, the two countries signed the Treaty of Tordesillas. The **treaty** created an imaginary line from the North Pole to the South Pole. Portugal was granted all lands "discovered" east of the line. Spain was granted all lands "discovered" west of the line. When Portuguese sea captain Pedro Álvares Cabral landed on the northeastern coast of Brazil on April 22, 1500, he was east of the line, so he claimed the land for Portugal.

Seeking natural resources

After exploring the coast, Cabral sent a ship back to Portugal to tell King Manuel I about the land he found. The king sent three ships to map this land and to look for natural resources. The explorers found valuable brazilwood trees, which were used to make a red dye. These trees became Brazil's first important **export**. In 1549, King João III, Manuel's son, declared Brazil a colony of Portugal. King João III sent officials to the town of Salvador, which became the capital of the colony, to run the government.

(top) Some rock paintings created by Brazil's indigenous people are thousands of years old. The woman on the right of this rock painting has a large, round stomach to show that she is expecting a baby.

Indigenous and African slaves

By the late 1500s, sugar cane was an important crop, especially in northeastern Brazil. Indigenous people were captured by adventurers called *bandeirantes* and forced to work as slaves on sugar cane **plantations**. Many died from the brutal work, while others were killed by diseases brought by the Europeans.

As demand for sugar increased in Europe, more slaves were needed to plant and harvest the crop, so traders began to bring slaves from many parts of Africa to work on the plantations. After *bandeirantes* discovered gold in the southeastern state of Minas Gerais in 1695 and in the western state of Mato Grosso in 1719, slaves were sent there to work in the mines. Between three and four million slaves were taken from Africa to Brazil before slavery was abolished in 1888.

Quilombos

Life for slaves on the plantations and in the mines was very difficult. Many African slaves risked their lives to escape. Some fled to the forests and set up slave retreats called *quilombos*. The largest *quilombo* was Palmares, on the border of the northeastern states of Alagoas and Pernambuco. Palmares, which was actually a group of *quilombos*, once had 20,000 residents. It was organized like many African tribes, with a king, royal council, army, and priest class.

Palmares was destroyed in 1694 by 2,000 slave hunters and *bandeirantes*. Many inhabitants who survived the attack starved themselves to death rather than returning to slavery. **Descendants** of the slaves still live in 724 communities that began as *quilombos*. In 2002, the Brazilian government granted the *quilombo* lands to the descendants of the original *quilombo* inhabitants.

This illustration from 1558 shows drawings of explorer ships sent from Portugal, some led by Pedro Álvares Cabral.

Gold and diamonds

By 1760, Brazil's mines were producing nearly half the world's gold. In 1729, diamonds were discovered in Minas Gerais. The city of Diamantina was built at the center of the diamond-mining area. Other settlements sprang up to provide goods and services to the miners. More than three million carats of diamonds came from Brazil's mines during the next 100 years. Profits from mining were used to begin coffee plantations. Coffee was Brazil's next important product.

African slaves collect coffee beans in the hot Brazilian sun, in this illustration from 1750.

African slaves worked long hours washing diamonds in mining camps, as in this illustration from the mid 1800s.

Tiradentes

Joaquim José da Silva Xavier (1748–1792) was an army officer and part-time dentist. His nickname, Tiradentes, means "toothpuller." Tiradentes and many others were angry that the Portuguese government demanded high taxes, but did not allow Brazilians to vote for their government. He led a movement to make Brazil independent of Portugal. In 1789, Tiradentes and ten others were arrested for plotting to overthrow the government. After a two-year trial, Tiradentes was found guilty of crimes against his country, and was hanged. Each year, on April 21, Brazilians celebrate Tiradentes Day to remember the first hero of Brazilian independence.

Princes and emperors

In 1822, Portuguese king Dom João VI put his son Dom Pedro in charge of Brazil. Dom Pedro, who was living in Brazil, declared the country's independence from Portugal and was crowned emperor. His rule was followed by that of his son, Dom Pedro II.

In 1888, while Dom Pedro II was in Europe, his daughter Isabel passed a law freeing the slaves. Slave owners were angry and, with the army, carried out a **coup** on November 15, 1889. They overthrew Dom Pedro II and declared Brazil a republic. Brazilians could now choose their country's president and their government. Slavery remained illegal.

The Republic of Brazil

Between 1889 and 1930, thirteen presidents were elected in Brazil. The government was in a state of chaos. In 1930, Getúlio Vargas, the governor of the southern state of Rio Grande do Sul, led a military coup and became president. He worked hard to help the poor and improve health care and education, but over time he became a **dictator**. In 1945, the military forced Vargas from power and restored democracy. Vargas was re-elected in 1951, but was unable to strengthen Brazil's economy. After a group of army officers demanded his resignation in 1954, Vargas committed suicide. When the next election was held in 1955, Juscelino Kubitschek was chosen president.

Many changes took place in Brazil during the rule of Dom Pedro II (1825–1891). The first paved road was built, the first steam engine started running, and telephones and postage stamps were used for the first time.

People in Rio de Janeiro welcome military troops that helped overthrow the government in 1930.

Juscelino Kubitschek

President Kubitschek promised "fifty years of progress in five." He kept his promise. Under his leadership, factories, roads, dams, and a new capital city, Brasília, were built. Brazil borrowed the enormous sums of money needed for these projects from international banks. The country's **debt** soared, prices of food and other goods skyrocketed, and salaries dropped. In 1964, the army took control of Brazil. Modernization continued, but people did not have the freedom to express their points of view. Those who opposed the military government were **exiled** or killed. In the 1980s, the economy slowed again, and Brazil could not repay its loans. International banks forced the Brazilian government to reduce its spending. Once again, wages fell, prices skyrocketed, and health care deteriorated.

Fernando Enrique Cardoso

The military was unable to resolve the country's economic problems, so it handed power back to an elected government in 1985. The situation did not improve until June 1994, when Finance Minister Fernando Enrique Cardoso introduced a new **currency**, the *real*, and a new plan to reduce **inflation**. His program, called the *Plano Real*, or *Real* Plan, also created jobs, lowered prices, and raised incomes. Cardoso was elected president in 1994 and was re-elected in 1998.

Brazil's currency, the real, is printed on thin sheets of plastic instead of paper. Plastic notes are cheaper to produce, and last four times as long as paper money.

In a special ceremony on April 21, 1960, President Juscelino Kubitschek, on the left, receives the key to the new Brazilian capital, Brasília.

9

Brazil's indigenous peoples

About 345,000 indigenous people live in villages in Brazil. They belong to 215 groups and speak 180 languages. Some lead traditional lives as hunters and gatherers. Others combine traditional and modern lifestyles, such as watching television in their rainforest homes. Many indigenous people have left their villages permanently to live in cities, and are no longer counted in the **census** as part of Brazil's indigenous population.

A woman from the village of A-Ukre, in the northern state of Pará, washes her child in the Amazon River.

The Guarani

The largest indigenous group in Brazil is the Guarani, numbering about 30,000 people. They live in the southwestern state of Mato Grosso do Sul and in the southeastern states of Paraná, São Paulo, Espirito Santo, and Rio de Janeiro. The Guarani work hard to preserve their traditional way of life, even though they have lost most of their lands to ranches and large farms. Parents teach their children how to fish, hunt, and grow crops such as **manioc**. They speak the Guarani language, but many children attend public schools where they also learn Portuguese. Religion is very important in Guarani communities. Each day begins and ends with prayer, dancing, and singing in celebration of "the great father," whom they call Nhanderú.

Ticuna

The Ticuna were one of the first groups that the Portuguese explorers met when they came to Brazil. Today, about 20,000 Ticuna live in the northwestern state of Amazonas, near Peru and Colombia. The Ticuna create beautiful handicrafts, such as baskets, masks, and wood and stone sculptures. They are also known for their colorful paintings on fabric made of bark.

A Ticuna girl smiles to show her teeth that are filed into points, a cultural tradition of her people.

Yawalapiti men practice huka-huka wrestling at their village in the Amazon rainforest. Behind the wrestlers is a communal hut, where the head of a family, his children, and his grandchildren live.

The Kayapó

About 4,000 Kayapó live in the southern part of the state of Pará. The center of a Kayapó village is the men's house, where boys go to live when they are eight years old. They stay in the men's house until their first child is six months old, then they move in with their wife and child. Other villagers' homes surround the men's house. A garden provides much of the village's food, including manioc and sweet potatoes. Women cook the food at a community oven.

In the 1980s, **logging** and mining threatened the Kayapó's way of life. Kayapó leaders gained international attention by making videos and writing articles about the threats to their land. This attention helped the Kayapó convince the Brazilian government to set aside 38,600 square miles (99,975 square kilometers) of land for their use. Some villages receive money for allowing outsiders to do limited logging and mining on their land.

A Kayapó man in traditional dress uses his video camera to film a movie.

Threats to indigenous people

Ranching, farming, logging, gold and iron ore mining, and dam and road construction have destroyed large parts of the rainforest. Indigenous people have been forced off their land, and many have died from diseases brought by outsiders. Since about 1910, the government has set aside protected areas in which indigenous people can live. In most cases, these areas are part of the indigenous people's traditional land.

In 1973, Brazil's indigenous people were granted legal rights to their traditional land and to their way of life. A formal process of demarcating, or setting aside, their land began. Then, in 1996, the government passed a law that made it possible for loggers, miners, and ranchers already on indigenous land to continue their activities while they challenged demarcation. Indigenous people are fighting in court to protect their rights, and are working to raise awareness about threats to their way of life and to the Amazon rainforest.

 # The Yanomami

According to a Yanomami myth, Omam, the god who created the world, caught a woman while fishing one day. Together, they had many children. These are the Yanomami people.

About 10,000 Yanomami live deep in Brazil's northern Amazon. Until the 1980s, they had very little contact with outsiders. Since then, large parts of their land have been taken over by miners looking for gold, by the military for army bases, and by ranchers clearing the land to graze cattle. In 1993, gold miners killed fourteen Yanomami men, women, and children, bringing worldwide attention to the Yanomami people. Today, groups of Yanomami who used to battle each other are working together to preserve their traditional way of life.

(top) A Yanomami girl inserts thin pieces of wood in her nose and lips, which the Yanomami believe resemble the whiskers of a cat.

Different roles

Yanomami men and women have very different roles. The men hunt giant anteaters, tapirs, armadillos, monkeys, wild boars, alligators, rodents, and birds. They make weapons and build *yanos*, large huts in which the villagers live. Young boys learn how to hunt and build a fire by watching the adults and older boys. They also learn to recognize animal tracks, clear the forest for a garden, and defend the village. When they turn fourteen, the boys are considered adults and join the men in the hunt.

Women plant and take care of crops such as sweet potatoes, manioc, and **plantain**. They also gather wild honey and fruits from the rainforest; weave hammocks, baskets, and nets; and make clothing. The young girls of the village play with the younger boys and other girls. They also learn from adult women how to plant and harvest crops, gather and prepare food, spin cotton, look after babies, and collect water and firewood.

The *yano*

The *yano* is a large doughnut-shaped hut made from poles cut from rainforest trees. More than 20 families live in a *yano*, sleeping in hammocks hung from the poles. In the middle of the *yano* is a large, open space in which adults hold celebrations and community events. Children play games in this area, including "jaguars and **prey**." Half the children pretend to be jaguars, while the other half imagine they are the jaguars' prey. The jaguars chase their prey, which escape up the *yano*'s high poles.

Clothing and decorations

Yanomami women and men wear very simple clothing. The men wear only narrow cotton waistbands. The women wear short, fringed cotton aprons and tops made of pieces of cotton that cross their chests. To add decoration, men add colorful feathers to their headdresses or armbands. Women wear woven cotton bands around their necks, waists, arms, and legs. Both men and women use red dye from *urucu* seeds and purple dye from fruit-palm juice to paint their faces and bodies with lines, spots, and squiggles. On special occasions, men paint themselves to look like jaguars, spider monkeys, and other rainforest animals.

A Yanomami village consists of several buildings called yanos. *The roof of a* yano *is made of overlapping palm leaves, with a hole in the center.*

Spiritual beliefs

Many of the Yanomami's spiritual beliefs involve *hekura*, which are the spirits of plants, animals, and elements of nature, such as the sun and the moon. A shaman, or healer, attracts *hekura* to live on his chest and lend him their powers. It is believed that the shaman and *hekura* work together to hold the land and sky in place, and to help the community. The shaman speaks to the *hekura* by falling into a **trance** and imitating the spirits with cries and gestures. The shaman must be careful not to displease the *hekura*; otherwise, the *hekura* will return to the forest and the shaman will lose the powers they gave him.

A Yanomami man tests his bow and arrow before a hunt. The black charcoal on his face represents courage.

Since the Portuguese arrived in Brazil in 1500, many people from around the world have inhabited the country. Some, such as the Africans, were brought by force to work as slaves. Others, including Japanese, Germans, and Italians, came willingly in search of a better life. Most Brazilians are descended from the Portuguese settlers, or are a mix of Portuguese, African, and indigenous people.

Portuguese influences

From the 1500s to the early 1800s, about 500,000 Portuguese people **immigrated** to Brazil. They established plantations and worked as merchants, hoping to become wealthy from the land's natural resources and fertile soil. After slavery was abolished in 1888, the demand for workers grew and another two million Portuguese came to the country. They brought their language, religion, and system of government with them. Their instruments, such as the small *taro* drum and large *surdo* drum, became part of Brazilian music, and their styles of **architecture**, including buildings with blue-patterned ceramic tiles, white stucco walls, and orange-tiled roofs, were seen in cities and villages throughout the land.

Some early Portuguese explorers moved inland, in the northeast, to raise cattle. Today, these cattle ranchers, called vaquieros, *wear leather chaps to protect their legs while riding horses.*

This Brazilian family spends the day in Manaus, a northern town deep in the rainforest.

From Africa

Most of the African slaves brought to Brazil were forced to work on plantations in the northeast. Others worked as servants, or were trained as carpenters, sculptors, and painters. When the slaves were freed in 1888, many stayed in the northeast. African music, food, and religious practices are very popular in this region, especially in Salvador. The best known form of Brazilian music, the *samba*, is a combination of Portuguese folk music and African tribal rhythms. Brazilian food is made from ingredients introduced by African slaves, such as coconut milk, palm oil, and hot peppers. Many people in the northeast follow African religions, including Macumba and Candomblé.

The full skirts worn by Baianas, or women from the northeastern state of Bahia, are made up of many layers of lacy material. Starch is sometimes added to the lace to make the layers stand out stiffly.

Recent immigrants

About 150 years ago, people from Italy, Spain, and Germany began immigrating to Brazil, in search of a better life. Many of these people settled in the south, where they worked on coffee plantations and established small farms. During the early 1900s, people from Eastern Europe, Russia, and Japan came to Brazil. They settled in São Paulo, which now has many ethnic neighborhoods, including Bela Vista, where more than a million residents of Italian descent live.

Poverty in Brazil

Many of Brazil's people are very poor. Organizations, such as the Movimento dos Trabalhadores Rurais Sem Terra (MST), or the Landless Workers Movement, assist people in need. Since 1985, the MST has organized "land invasions" to help many of Brazil's 4.8 million landless families. Under Brazilian law, the government can purchase unused land and give it to the landless, but it often does not do so. The MST helps people settle on unused farms and pastures; establish cooperative farms, where people share in the work and profits; and build schools and medical clinics. More than 1,000 people settled by MST have been killed by ranchers and landowners, but 250,000 families have been granted land, while more than 70,000 are still waiting for the government to acknowledge their right to the land.

A Japanese woman stands outside her flower shop in the São Paulo neighborhood of Liberdade, the largest Japanese community outside Japan.

 # Work and play in cities

Brazil's busy cities are places of work and play. Buses, subways, cars, and **trolleys** rush through the streets. Hungry city dwellers stop at *lanchonetes*, or snack bars, for a quick hamburger, pastry, or freshly squeezed fruit drink. On the beaches of coastal cities, people swim, read, and play soccer. Fruit sellers walk around with fresh pineapples and coconuts that they slice open with a knife. Other vendors sell soft drinks, ice cream, hats, swimsuits, kites, and mats on which to lie.

City industry

Brazil's cities are industrial centers. Factories owned by Ford, General Motors, and Volkswagen make cars and trucks. IBM and Microsoft produce computer hardware and software. Other companies manufacture electrical appliances, such as refrigerators, washing machines, televisions, and radios. Brazil also has a large shoe and fabric industry. Enormous ships dock in the ports of Salvador, Rio de Janeiro, and Santos, near São Paulo, ready to pick up and drop off cargo. Almost half of all the goods produced in Brazil for export are shipped from Santos, Brazil's main port.

(top) Miles of sandy beaches are within walking distance of high-rise offices, apartment buildings, and hotels in Salvador.

(left) People stop for a cold drink at a suco stand in Rio de Janeiro. Sucos are made with fruit, such as passionfruit or limes, blended with ice.

A place to call home

The downtown areas of Brazilian cities have many high-rise buildings, mostly with small apartments. They are home to the growing middle class of teachers, health care workers, and government employees. In the **suburbs**, people live in low-rise apartment buildings and small wood or brick houses. The suburbs also have areas of single-story homes with enclosed gardens, and luxurious mansions where wealthy people live. The mansions are surrounded by high gates and are often protected by armed guards.

Favelas

Many people from Brazil's countryside have moved to cities in search of a better life. Most cities do not have enough hospitals, schools, or homes for everyone, and people must live in

One of the largest favelas in Brazil is Rocinha, on a hill in Rio de Janeiro. More than 150,000 people live in homes packed onto this hill.

favelas, or shantytowns. Brazil has more than 3,500 *favelas*. People who live there build one-room homes out of corrugated iron, wood, cardboard, and sometimes bricks and cement. cement. Many *favelas* do not have running water, electricity, a sewage system, or garbage collection.

Abandonados

It is estimated that seven to eight million abandoned children, or *abandonados*, live on the streets of Brazil's cities. Most of these *meninos de rua*, or street children, were abandoned by parents who could not afford to feed, clothe, and house them. Others were abused or neglected by their parents, and ran away from home. They sleep in doorways and alleys, sometimes huddled together for warmth and comfort. To survive, they beg for money, sell candy or fruit on street corners, or steal. Organizations such as Casa de Passagem, or Passage House, in the northeastern city of Recife, provide *abandonados* with food, education, and a safe place to sleep.

A rubber tapper turns latex into rubber by heating it in a pot over a fire. Another way to make rubber is to add a chemical called acetic acid to harden the latex and then press it into blocks.

Brazil's indigenous people were the first people to live in the rainforest. They learned to use the animals and plants of the forest for food, medicine, clothing, shelter, musical instruments, and decorations. Over time, people of mixed Portuguese and African background moved to the rainforest to hunt, fish, or farm.

Since the 1800s, people in the rainforest have also worked as rubber tappers. They cut v-shaped notches into rubber trees and let a milky liquid called latex drip into cups, which they collect at the end of the day. In 1966, a government plan known as "Operation Amazonia" brought even more people to the rainforest to work on farms and ranches, to build roads, and to work in mining and logging operations. These newcomers have cleared large areas of rainforest that scientists estimate will take 300 years to restore.

Farming fragile soil

Indigenous people and others who have lived in the rainforest for a long time farm the thin, ancient soil in ways that do not destroy it. They use a method of farming called "slash and burn." First, they clear a small section of the forest using axes and long knives called machetes. Then, they burn everything that they slashed. The ash from the burned plants and trees fertilizes the soil.

Secrets of the rainforest

Many plants in the rainforest are used for medicines. Shamans, or traditional medicine people, know that the sap from a palm tree stops the bleeding of a severe cut, and that the leaves of the *pata de vaca* tree balance blood sugar levels in people with diabetes. More than 100 **pharmaceutical** companies are studying medicinal plants used by shamans. Some companies have earned enormous profits from medicines made from rainforest plants, but they have not paid the indigenous people a fair amount for their knowledge. This practice of taking information without paying the people who have the knowledge is referred to as "biopiracy." The governments of some Amazon states, such as the northwestern state of Acre, have passed laws to stop biopiracy.

Flooding is a problem for people who live close to rivers. They often build their homes on stilts or wooden platforms, or live on rafts or houseboats.

Hunting

Hunters stalk through the rainforest, hoping to return home with a giant anteater, tapir, parrot, or toucan. Indigenous hunters often catch game with bows and arrows or blowguns. A blowgun is made from a hollow bamboo stem. Inside is a dart dipped in a poison called curare. The dart is released by blowing air through the gun's stem. Many indigenous people also hunt with shotguns, as other people in the rainforest do.

Fishing

Fishers along the Amazon's many rivers search for quiet pools where fish such as peacock bass, *arawanas*, and *payara* gather. Most fishers use hooks and nets, but some use poison. They brush *ayori-toto* vines, which contain a poisonous sap, through the water, stunning the fish. When the stunned fish rise to the surface, the fishers quickly grab them before the poison wears off. The *ayori-toto* vines do not contaminate the rivers because the poison soon loses its effect.

Getting around the rainforest

Traditionally, people in the rainforest paddled down the river in *ubás*, which are dugout canoes. They made these canoes by hollowing out trees and placing wooden boards across the insides to stretch the canoes into just the right shape. Today, many people attach motors to their canoes to travel faster. Larger boats can also be seen on the Amazon.

On land, people drive along the Trans-Amazon Highway. Parts of the highway are paved, while other parts are just dirt tracks. In places where the highway is broken up by a river, cars and buses cross by ferry.

Jivaro men, living in the Amazon rainforest, practice shooting blowguns before a hunt. The slender poison darts inside the blowguns seem breakable, but they can easily pierce a tree.

At the age of fifteen, a girl is considered an adult. A special party, called Festa dos Quinze Anos, *is held for her, with dinner, dancing, and a cake.*

Special celebrations and ceremonies mark births, passages from youth to adulthood, marriages, deaths, and other stages in the lives of Brazilians. Most Brazilian children who are Catholic are baptized. During a baptism, a priest sprinkles holy water over the baby's head as a symbol of washing away sin and making him or her a member of the Catholic Church.

Happy birthday to you

Loud choruses of *"Parabéns a Você,"* the Brazilian version of "Happy Birthday," ring out at birthday parties in Brazil. At many parties, children play games and dress in costumes related to a theme, such as cartoon characters, stuffed animals, or nature. At other parties, they are entertained by clowns or magicians, or they play on trampolines. Popular party foods include appetizers, such as codfish balls and fried sausage, and sweets, including chocolate balls rolled in coconut or sprinkles and wrapped in colorful paper.

After a wedding, guests throw rice outside the church to celebrate the newly married couple.

From child to adult

Many indigenous people hold special ceremonies, or initiation **rites**, when a young person becomes an adult. For one month, young Munduruku males live in the men's house with their fathers and godfathers, who teach them to hunt, fish, and survive in the rainforest. Then, they must pass a test to prove that they are mature, courageous, and ready to become adults. They head deep into the forest to catch an animal large enough to feed the whole village. The test is difficult, and not all young men pass on the first try.

Getting married

Many Brazilians celebrate weddings in similar ways to North Americans, with a religious ceremony, elaborate dinner, and dancing. The marriage customs and rituals of indigenous people can be very simple. Marriages are often arranged when the bride and groom are children. For several years, the boy has to hunt, garden, and do other work for the girl's father to prove that he is responsible. Then, when it is time for the marriage, the groom just moves his belongings to the bride's home and ties his hammock next to hers.

Funerals

When Brazilians of Portuguese background die, their family holds a *velório* to honor their memory. Traditionally, the *velório* was held at home. Mourners visited for the whole night and told stories about the person who died. Today, many people hold the *velório* in a funeral home or church. The burial usually takes place within twenty-four hours of the death, and a special Mass to remember the person is held one week, one month, and one year after the death. For 49 days after a Brazilian of Japanese descent dies, friends and family visit the deceased's home where it is believed the person's spirit rests. After the 49th day, they believe the person's spirit goes to heaven.

A ceremony of mourning

The Yanomami wrap the body of a person who has died in a bundle of sticks and place it on a high platform in the forest. Several weeks later, when the body has decomposed, or broken down, they clean the skeleton and burn it, and begin to prepare for a special ceremony of mourning. During the ceremony, the deceased's family mixes the ashes of the deceased person with bananas and water. Then, they drink the mixture. The Yanomami believe that once they drink all the ashes and destroy all the person's belongings, the person's spirit can move on to the next world.

The Yanomami people also believe that after a family member dies, it is bad luck to mention that person's name again, so babies are given names that have never been used in the family. Many of these names are very specific, such as words that in English mean "whisker of the howler monkey" or "toenail of the sloth."

Kalapalo dancers, wearing jingling ankle bells, dance at a ceremony for the dead in Xingu National Park, in the north. The ceremony marks the death of a member of the chief's family.

A girl plays educational games on the computer at her school in Rio de Janeiro.

Brazilian children are required to attend school from the age of seven to fourteen, although some children leave school early to help their families earn money. Most children attend public schools that are run by the government, but there are also church-run schools and private schools for children of wealthier families. Communities in remote areas sometimes start their own schools. These schools often have just one small room where a teacher instructs children of all ages.

The school day

Most Brazilian children begin school at 7:00 a.m. with the singing of the national anthem, *O Hino Nacional*, and end at 1:00 p.m., when they return home for lunch. Students in areas that do not have enough schools attend classes in shifts, from 7:00 a.m. to 11:30 a.m. or from 1:00 p.m. to 5:30 p.m. After the fifth grade, schools offer evening classes for students who work during the day. For all students, summer vacation is in January and February, which is winter in North America. Seasons in Brazil are the opposite of seasons in North America because most of Brazil lies south of the **equator**, while North America is north of the equator.

Rubber tappers' children often attend one-room schools in the rainforest, such as this school in the northwestern state of Acre.

From one year to the next

Children go to primary school, or *primeiro grau*, for eight years, taking subjects such as mathematics, science, social studies, Portuguese, English, and physical education. During their midmorning break, called *intervalo*, they eat snacks and play games such as *amarelinha*, or hopscotch; *esconde-esconde*, or hide and seek; and *pique-pega*, or tag. Children also play singing games and games where they try to capture each other's kites. During their three years in high school, or *segundo grau*, students either take courses to prepare for college, such as chemistry, physics, and geography, or courses to prepare for a job after high school.

A Kanamari man learns Portuguese at a Catholic-run school for indigenous people, in the northwestern state of Amazonas.

Passing the *vestibular*

Students usually complete high school when they are seventeen years old. If they want to go to college or university, they must pass a difficult test called the *vestibular*, which takes two or three days to write. Each year, usually in January or June, students cram into lecture halls, gyms, and even soccer stadiums to be tested in biology, chemistry, physics, math, Portuguese, English, and other subjects. For months leading up to the *vestibular*, students study for hours each day, and usually have no time for other activities. Some even spend a whole year attending *cursinhos*, special courses that help them prepare for the exam.

Education of indigenous peoples

In the past, many indigenous people went to schools run by **missionaries**. Today, some schools are still run by religious missions, but others are run by the government and by national and international organizations. Indigenous students learn the same subjects as other students in Brazil, as well as indigenous languages, history, crafts, and the skills needed to survive in the rainforest. Some children also attend council meetings and debating sessions in their village, where they learn from elders about the group's way of life.

These students work with a teacher to pass the vestibular and continue their education.

Fun and games

On Brazil's many long, sandy beaches, people swim, surf, sail, hang glide, and play volleyball and soccer. Some play paddleball, hitting a rubber ball back and forth to a friend with a paddle. Others use their bare hands to hit a *peteca* to a partner. A *peteca* is a ball of sand that is wrapped in leather and has feathers attached. Those who want a challenge play *futevolei*. *Futevolei* is like beach volleyball, except players cannot use their hands. Instead, they use their feet and heads, as in soccer.

Friends play futevolei, *a sport that combines soccer and volleyball, on Flamengo Beach in Rio de Janeiro.*

Soccer in the streets and stadiums

Soccer, or *futebol* as Brazilians call it, was introduced to Brazil in 1884, and is now the country's favorite sport. People play it everywhere: in parks, on streets, and on beaches. There is even a version of soccer in which players in trucks push a huge soccer ball into the opposing team's giant net.

Thousands of Brazilian fans attended this Women's World Cup soccer match between Brazil and Germany.

Brazilians love to watch their favorite professional soccer teams on TV or in stadiums, where they paint themselves in team colors and scream out cheers. After a victory, Brazilians celebrate with fireworks and street parties. Brazilians have had many reasons to celebrate. Brazil has won five World Cup championships, more than any other country. The World Cup is an international soccer tournament played every four years.

Pelé

Edson Arantes do Nascimento is better known around the world as Pelé. Born in 1940, he became one of the best soccer players ever. He helped Brazil win three World Cup championships, and over his eighteen-year career with Brazil's national team, he scored more than 1,200 goals. Although he retired in 1977, Pelé is still known throughout Brazil as Rei Pelé, the king of soccer.

Two athletes practice capoeira *near the ocean in Salvador. There are many* capoeira *schools throughout Brazil, especially in Salvador, where people learn this challenging art.*

Capoeira

Capoeira began as a martial art practiced by African slaves in northeastern Brazil. Owners saw the strength, confidence, and fighting skills that their slaves gained through *capoeira*, and soon forbade the martial art. To disguise what they were doing, the slaves changed *capoeira* so that it looked like an acrobatic dance. Two slaves kicked and leaped in time to a *berimbau*, a one-stringed instrument which a third slave played. Today, *capoeira* participants perform cartwheels and whirling handstands across the floor, trying to knock their opponents off balance with their heads, legs, and feet, while still looking graceful.

Fast cars

Brazil is known for its world-class race car drivers. Rubens Barrichello and Cristiano da Motta are following in the footsteps of Brazil's racing legends: Nelson Piquet, Ayrton Senna, and Emerson Fittipaldi. Piquet participated in many international Grand Prix races, winning the first of his three World Championships in 1981.

Ayrton Senna was one of the world's best racers, having won three World Championships before he was killed during a Grand Prix race in 1994. Emerson Fittipaldi, called "Emmo" by his fans, was the youngest Formula 1 World Champion in history. He was just 25 years old when he won the first of his three World Championships. Then, Fittipaldi switched to IndyCar racing, and won the Indianapolis 500 twice.

Telenovelas

Many Brazilians cannot wait to find out what will happen to the characters on their favorite evening soap operas, or *telenovelas*. *Telenovelas* are shown on TV six nights a week and last for up to eight months. They can be serious, funny, or both, and are usually based on politics, families, and social problems such as poverty and **racism**. In stores, on the beach, and at home, people gossip about the characters, and argue about which show is the best. Television networks even ask viewers what they would like to happen in the shows, then they add the viewers' ideas to the *telenovelas*.

Delicious dishes

Each group of people in Brazil introduced different foods and ways of cooking to the country. The indigenous people introduced fresh fruits, such as the camu-camu fruit, which has purplish-red skin and yellow pulp; nuts, such as the three-cornered Brazil nut; and manioc. The Portuguese brought beans, rice, sugar cane, and coffee. Africans introduced bananas, hot peppers, and a type of palm oil called *dendê*. People from Germany brought sausages, *schnitzel*, which is a thin slice of veal or other meat, and a type of pastry called *strudel*. The Japanese brought *sushi*, which is raw fish served over rice or wrapped with rice in seaweed.

A vendor prepares food to be sold to a hungry lunch crowd at an outdoor market.

To market, to market

Some Brazilians shop for food in supermarkets. Others prefer to shop in outdoor markets, where rows of vendors sell fresh fruit, vegetables, cheese, chicken, eggs, fish, and prepared foods. Shoppers are invited to sample the produce to make sure it is fresh and tasty. After a few hours, they return home with straw bags or shopping carts filled with their purchases.

A Yanomami girl peels manioc plants. The indigenous people of Brazil were the first to discover that manioc can be eaten after it is processed, although it is poisonous when raw.

Daily meals

Many Brazilians start the day with a light breakfast of *café com leite*, or hot milk and coffee, and a slice of fresh bread covered in jam. Sometimes, people also eat ham, cheese, and fresh fruit. Lunch is served around noon and is normally the largest meal of the day. It can take two hours to eat and usually includes rice, beans, meat, and a salad, followed by fresh fruit or another dessert. Brazilians eat a light dinner of *café com leite*, bread, cheese, fried plantain, and cold cuts at about 7:30 p.m.

Made with manioc

Every day, Brazilians eat products made from the root of the manioc plant. Indigenous people peel, chop, and squeeze the root in a sieve to get rid of a poisonous acid. Then, they eat the root after boiling it for many hours or they make a dry, spongy cracker-like bread, called *beiju*, from grated manioc.

Manioc products used by non-indigenous people are processed in factories, where the poisonous acid is removed by machines. *Farinha de mandioca* is a coarse, cornmeal-like grain which people sprinkle over rice, beans, meat, and fish or fry in a pan with a little butter to make a side dish called *farofa*. Manioc root can also be ground into a very fine flour, called *povilho*, which is baked into small rolls or used to make cakes and cookies.

Moqueca *is a stew made with shrimp and other fish that is cooked in a tomato sauce and seasoned with* malagueta *peppers,* dendê, *onions, and garlic.*

Carne de sol, *or dried salted meat, is popular in the hot, dry northeast because it can last for a long time without refrigeration. Salt is rubbed into the beef, then the beef is hung on racks to dry in the sun and wind.*

Feijoada

Brazil's national dish is a stew called *feijoada*. The original recipe came from African slaves, whose owners only fed them meat that they did not want to eat, such as pigs' feet, tails, or tongues. The slaves cooked these meats in a pot with onions, garlic, and other spices. Today, people eat a type of *feijoada* similar to the one that slaves ate. *Feijoada típica* is a stew with black beans, bacon, smoked sausage, salted beef, and pigs' ears and tails. It is usually served with bowls of boiled rice, orange slices, shredded *couve*, or **collard greens**, and *farofa*.

Beef and more beef

Each region of Brazil has its own foods that are prepared in special ways. In the south, where cattle are raised, people eat *churrasco*, which are skewers of beef seasoned with sea salt and roasted over hot coals. Fresh tomato and onion sauce is poured on top. *Churrasco* is usually served with rice, fried cornmeal or *farofa*, and sometimes a fried banana. At *churrasco* restaurants, called *rodízios*, waiters carry *churrasco* meats on large skewers to the tables. *Churrasco* also refers to a backyard barbecue where chicken, fish, sausage, and beef are grilled over hot coals.

Street vendors in cities throughout Brazil sell treats such as acarajé, *fried balls of peeled* fradinho beans *mashed with salt and onions. Inside the balls is* vatapá, *dried shrimp, pepper, and diced tomatoes.*

Thirsty cariocas, *as the people of Rio de Janeiro are called, often cool down with a* coco gelado. *Vendors cut off the top of a cold coconut, stick a straw inside, and customers drink the coconut water.*

African flavors

In the northeast, around Salvador, the food has a spicy, African flavor. Many dishes are made with *dendê*, coconut milk, fish, such as dried shrimp, squid, and crabmeat, and a spicy chili pepper called *malagueta*. *Vatapá* is a stew that is usually made with seafood, but can also be made with chicken. It is mixed with *dendê*, coconut, ground peanuts, and chopped green peppers. *Caruru* is made by boiling shrimp and okra, a popular Brazilian vegetable, then spicing the mixture with onions, peppers, and *dendê*.

In the Amazon and beyond

People in the Amazon eat a lot of fish, including *pirarucu* and *tucunaré*. These fish are served with *tucupi*, a sauce made from the juice of the manioc root. *Tucupi* is also used in *tacacá*, or shrimp soup, where it is mixed with tapioca gum, which thickens the soup, and *jambu* leaves. *Jambu* leaves contain an acid that causes people's tongue and lips to tingle. In the southeast, many dishes are made with pork; vegetables, such as *couve*; and *tutu*, a thick bean sauce made by grinding uncooked beans with manioc flour.

Thirsty?

Brazilians drink a lot of coffee, which they grow on their country's plantations. *Cafezinho*, which means "little coffee," is a strong type of coffee served in very small cups. *Gaúchos*, or cowboys in the south, drink *chimarrão*, also called *mate* tea. It is made from the leaves of the *erva mate* plant. *Gaúchos* pour the tea in a **gourd** and sip it through a straw.

With all of Brazil's fresh fruit, fruit drinks are very popular. *Suco* bars sell drinks made with ice, sugar, and fruit, such as mangoes, passionfruit, and *acerolas*, a round, tart fruit about the size of a blueberry. *Vitaminas*, which are made with fruit, milk, and sugar, are also popular. Brazil's national drink is *capirinha*. It is made by mixing *cachaça*, or rum made from sugar cane, with crushed lime and sugar.

Quindim

Brazilians make many sweets with coconut. *Quindim* is a sticky cake made from coconut and eggs. You can make it quickly and easily with an adult's help.

A vendor in Salvador pushes stalks of sugar cane through a machine to produce a sweet juice.

What you need:
1 cup (250 ml) sugar
1 cup (250 ml) grated coconut
1 tablespoon (15 ml) butter or margarine
large bowl
electric mixer
5 egg yolks
1 egg white, beaten until stiff
9-inch (22-centimeter) pie pan, greased with butter or margarine
roasting pan

What to do:
1. Preheat the oven to 350° Fahrenheit (175° Celsius).
2. Combine the sugar, coconut, and butter in the bowl.
3. Beat with the mixer, while adding the egg yolks one at a time.
4. Add the egg white and mix again.
5. Pour the mixture into the greased pie pan.
6. Place the pie pan in a roasting pan with 1 inch (2.5 centimeters) of boiling water at the bottom.
7. Bake for 30 minutes until golden brown.
8. Cool, then turn the pan upside down to remove the pie.

This recipe makes twelve slices.

Gabriela wakes up early Monday morning to the smell of fresh baking. She and her family are visiting Gabriela's godmother, or *madrinha*, and godfather, or *padrinho*, in Salvador.

Gabriela goes into the kitchen and sees that her mother, Cristina; father, Alexandro; and sister, Isabela, have been up for a while. The kitchen table is covered with delicious food: *bôlo de mandioca*, a breakfast cake made with manioc; *pão doce com queijo*, a type of Danish pastry with cheese; fresh slices of pineapple and mango; orange juice; and *café com leite*. Analúcia, Gabriela's *madrinha*, works in the kitchen of a hotel and is a wonderful cook.

As they eat, they discuss their plans for the day. "I have a surprise for you," says Sérgio, Gabriela's *padrinho*. "We are going to see Paulo play at the *capoeira* school." Paulo is a musician who plays the *berimbau*, and he is Sérgio's best friend. Gabriela is excited, but Isabela has something else in mind. "What about the Candomblé ceremony?" she asks. "Don't worry," Sérgio assures her. "We will go to the *capoeira* school this morning and to the Candomblé ceremony tonight."

After breakfast, everyone takes the bus to the *capoeira* school. Paulo has invited them to watch the dancers practice. Isabela looks worried as the dancers kick in the air and do cartwheels and somersaults. "Are they going to hurt each other? It looks like they are fighting." "Don't worry," laughs Sérgio. "They are only trying to knock each other off balance."

During a break, Paulo comes over to Gabriela. "*Bom dia*, Gabriela. Would you like to play the *berimbau*?" "*Sim*," she replies as she takes the instrument that accompanies the dancers. "You are a natural," remarks Paulo, as Gabriela holds a coin against the *berimbau*'s string and strikes it with the stick Paulo gave her.

Gabriela is excited to explore all the sights, sounds, and tastes of Salvador with her godparents.

After they leave the school, Cristina suggests they walk around the Cidade Alta, or Upper City. It is the historic part of Salvador, with gold-covered churches and mansions built during the 1600s and 1700s. Salvador's architecture is very different from the architecture of São Paulo. When Gabriela visits her father at work downtown, she is surrounded by tall buildings made of glass and steel.

The Catedral Basílica is one of many churches in Salvador. Tourists visit Salvador's churches to admire their beautiful paintings and tilework.

As they walk, Cristina, who grew up in Salvador but moved to São Paulo when she married Alexandro, describes some of the places she remembers from her childhood. "This is the Catedral Basílica, or Cathedral of Bahia," she tells them. "It was built between 1657 and 1672. The walls are made of marble, and the **altar** is made of marble and gold leaf." They keep walking until Cristina sees the Palácio do Rio Branco. "When Brazil was a Portuguese colony, the governor lived here," she explains. "Those plaster eagles were added later in the 1800s."

Analúcia sees a *Baiana*, as the women of the state of Bahia are called, selling *acarajé*. "*Tenho fome*," she says. It's time to eat. They all buy the fried balls of mashed beans, salt, onions, *vatapá*, shrimp, pepper, and diced tomatoes. Afterward, they return home for an afternoon nap, before Analúcia goes to work.

After catching up on all the news and eating a dinner of ham, cheese, and fresh fruit, Gabriela, Isabela, Cristina, Alexandro, and Sérgio go to the Candomblé ceremony. Tonight is a special night — a festival dedicated to Omulu, the god of plague and disease, to whom people pray for protection from illness.

When they arrive at the Casa Branca, where the ceremony takes place, the dancing has already begun. Everyone watches the women in their lace and hooped skirts move their hands gracefully and sway their hips back and forth while taking light steps. They chant to the rhythm of African drums, played by the men. After the ceremony, sweets, including *quindim*, are offered to everyone. Cristina and Alexandro notice that their daughters are getting tired, so they head back to Analúcia and Sérgio's for a good night's sleep.

Women participating in a Candomblé ceremony wear fancy costumes, bangle bracelets, and a beaded veil that covers their eyes.

31

Glossary

altar A table or stand used for religious ceremonies

archaeologist A person who studies the past by looking at buildings and artifacts

architecture The science and art of designing and constructing buildings

census An official count of a country's population

collard greens The leaves of kale, an edible plant

colonize To establish and control a settlement in a distant country

coup The overthrow of a government

currency Money

debt Money owed to another country

descendant A person who can trace his or her family roots to a certain family or group

dictator A ruler with complete power

economic Relating to the way a country organizes and manages its businesses, industries, and money

equator An imaginary line around the earth's center

exiled Forced from one's native country

export A product sold to another country

fertile Able to produce abundant crops or vegetation

gourd The hard-shelled fruit of certain vines

immigrate To move to another country

indigenous Native to a country

inflation A continuous increase in prices

logging The cutting down of forests

manioc A starchy root vegetable

missionary A person who travels to a foreign country to spread a particular religion

natural resource A material found in nature, such as oil, coal, minerals, or timber

pharmaceutical Related to the production of medicines

plain A large area of flat land

plantain A tropical fruit resembling a banana

plantation A large farm on which crops such as cotton and sugar are grown

plateau An area of flat land that is higher than the surrounding land

prey An animal hunted by another animal for food

racism The act of treating someone unfairly based on one's ethnic group

rite A ceremony that involves a set of fixed actions

suburb A residential area outside a city

trance A mental state during which people are not aware of what is happening around them

treaty A formal agreement signed by two or more countries

trolley An electric vehicle that moves on metal tracks in the road

Index

1 2 3 4 5 6 7 8 9 0   Printed in the USA   0 9 8 7 6 5 4 3

Franklin Pierce College Library

00145340

DATE DUE

DEC 1 2 2008 Iu# 40

MAR 2 8 2011

GAYLORD

PRINTED IN U.